MCR

JUN - 5 2007

EVANSTON PUBLIC LIBRARY

S0-ASG-261

JBegin First Rhymes
Scheunemann, Pam,
The frog in the clog /

DATE DUE

OCT 0 5 2007	
OCT 2 8 2007	
DEC 0 8 2007	
JAN 3 0 2008	
APR 1 7 2008	
9 2008	
APR 2 9 2008	

The Frog
in the Clog

Pam Scheunemann

Consulting Editor, Diane Craig, M.A./Reading Specialist

EVANSTON PUBLIC LIBRARY
CHILDREN'S DEPARTMENT
1703 ORRINGTON AVENUE
EVANSTON, ILLINOIS 60201

Published by ABDO Publishing Company, 4940 Viking Drive, Edina, Minnesota 55435.

Copyright © 2006 by Abdo Consulting Group, Inc. International copyrights reserved in all countries. No part of this book may be reproduced in any form without written permission from the publisher. SandCastle™ is a trademark and logo of ABDO Publishing Company.

Printed in the United States.

Credits
Edited by: Pam Price
Curriculum Coordinator: Nancy Tuminelly
Cover and Interior Design and Production: Mighty Media
Photo Credits: AbleStock, Photodisc

Library of Congress Cataloging-in-Publication Data

Scheunemann, Pam, 1955-
    The frog in the clog / Pam Scheunemann.
        p. cm. -- (First rhymes)
    Includes index.
    ISBN 1-59679-483-6 (hardcover)
    ISBN 1-59679-484-4 (paperback)
        1. English language--Rhyme--Juvenile literature. I. Title. II. Series.
PE1517.S426 2006
808.1--dc22

                                                                    2005048790

SandCastle™ books are created by a professional team of educators, reading specialists, and content developers around five essential components that include phonemic awareness, phonics, vocabulary, text comprehension, and fluency. All books are written, reviewed, and leveled for guided reading and early intervention reading, and designed for use in shared, guided, and independent reading and writing activities to support a balanced approach to literacy instruction.

Let Us Know

After reading the book, SandCastle would like you to tell us your stories about reading. What is your favorite page? Was there something hard that you needed help with? Share the ups and downs of learning to read. We want to hear from you! To get posted on the ABDO Publishing Company Web site, send us e-mail at:

sandcastle@abdopub.com

SandCastle Level: Beginning

-og

clog

dog

frog

hog

log

Here is a  .

He is a .

This is a .

This is a  .

This is a  .

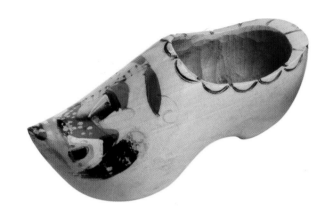

This clog is yellow.

The dog is white.

The frog is green.

The hog is big.

The log is thick.

The Frog
in the Clog

Once there was
a little dog.

Bog

The little dog
sat on a big log.

While the little dog
sat on the big log,
a very fat hog
came along from
the bog.

Bog 1 mile ←

The fat hog
gave a yellow clog
to the little dog
who sat on the big log.

Bog 1

Out of the yellow clog
jumped a little
green frog.

When the dog
saw the frog,
he fell off of the log!

About SandCastle™

A professional team of educators, reading specialists, and content developers created the SandCastle™ series to support young readers as they develop reading skills and strategies and increase their general knowledge. The SandCastle™ series has four levels that correspond to early literacy development in young children. The levels are provided to help teachers and parents select the appropriate books for young readers.

Emerging Readers
(no flags)

Beginning Readers
(1 flag)

Transitional Readers
(2 flags)

Fluent Readers
(3 flags)

These levels are meant only as a guide. All levels are subject to change.

ABDO
Publishing Company

To see a complete list of SandCastle™ books and other nonfiction titles from ABDO Publishing Company, visit **www.abdopub.com** or contact us at:
4940 Viking Drive, Edina, Minnesota 55435 • 1-800-800-1312 • fax: 1-952-831-1632